50 Easter Eats
Recipes for Home

By: Kelly Johnson

Table of Contents

- Honey Glazed Ham
- Roast Lamb with Mint Sauce
- Deviled Eggs with Smoked Salmon
- Hot Cross Buns
- Spinach and Feta Stuffed Mushrooms
- Lemon Herb Roasted Chicken
- Asparagus and Prosciutto Bundles
- Scalloped Potatoes
- Caprese Salad Skewers
- Baked Salmon with Dill Sauce
- Carrot Ginger Soup
- Pesto Deviled Eggs
- Garlic Rosemary Roasted Lamb
- Spring Pea Risotto
- Shrimp Cocktail
- Raspberry Almond Tart
- Easter Bunny Cupcakes
- Grilled Vegetable Platter
- Apricot Glazed Roast Chicken
- Bacon-Wrapped Asparagus
- Lemon Blueberry Cheesecake
- Greek Salad
- Raspberry Lemon Muffins
- Stuffed Bell Peppers with Quinoa
- Chocolate Covered Strawberries
- Roasted Vegetable Quiche
- Easter Nest Cookies
- Broccoli and Cheddar Casserole
- Mint Chocolate Chip Ice Cream Cake
- Smoked Salmon Platter
- Spring Pea and Mint Pesto Pasta
- Orange Glazed Carrots
- Mini Quiches
- Easter Egg Sugar Cookies
- Honey Mustard Glazed Chicken

- Cucumber Avocado Salad
- Lemon Sorbet
- Baked Ziti with Ricotta and Spinach
- Raspberry Lemonade Punch
- Pecan-Crusted Rack of Lamb
- Creamy Mushroom and Spinach Tart
- Lemon Poppy Seed Muffins
- Roasted Asparagus with Parmesan
- Easter Bunny Cake
- Teriyaki Glazed Salmon
- Spring Vegetable Stir-Fry
- Strawberry Shortcake
- Lemon Garlic Butter Shrimp
- Raspberry Lemonade Cupcakes
- Maple Glazed Roasted Carrots

Honey Glazed Ham

Ingredients:

- 1 bone-in, fully cooked ham (8-10 pounds)
- 1 cup honey
- 1/2 cup Dijon mustard
- 1/4 cup brown sugar
- 1/4 cup orange juice
- 1 teaspoon ground cloves
- 1 teaspoon ground cinnamon

Instructions:

Preheat your oven to 325°F (163°C).
Place the ham in a roasting pan, cut side down.
In a saucepan over medium heat, combine honey, Dijon mustard, brown sugar, orange juice, ground cloves, and ground cinnamon. Stir the mixture until the ingredients are well combined and the honey and sugar have dissolved.
Bring the glaze to a simmer and cook for 5-7 minutes, allowing it to thicken slightly.
Brush a generous amount of the honey glaze over the entire surface of the ham, using a pastry brush.
Cover the ham with aluminum foil, tenting it slightly to prevent the foil from sticking to the glaze.
Bake the ham in the preheated oven, allowing approximately 15-20 minutes of cooking time per pound. Baste the ham with the honey glaze every 30 minutes.
During the last 15-20 minutes of baking, remove the foil to allow the ham to caramelize and develop a golden crust.
Once the internal temperature of the ham reaches 140°F (60°C), remove it from the oven.
Let the ham rest for 15-20 minutes before carving.
Slice the ham and serve with the remaining honey glaze as a drizzle or dipping sauce.

Enjoy your delicious Honey Glazed Ham as a centerpiece for your Easter feast or any special occasion!

Roast Lamb with Mint Sauce

Ingredients:

For the Roast Lamb:

- 1 leg of lamb (5-7 pounds), bone-in
- 4 cloves garlic, minced
- 2 tablespoons fresh rosemary, chopped
- 2 tablespoons fresh thyme, chopped
- 2 tablespoons olive oil
- Salt and black pepper to taste

For the Mint Sauce:

- 1 cup fresh mint leaves, finely chopped
- 1/4 cup white sugar
- 1/2 cup boiling water
- 1/2 cup white wine vinegar

Instructions:

For the Roast Lamb:

> Preheat your oven to 325°F (163°C).
> In a small bowl, combine minced garlic, chopped rosemary, chopped thyme, olive oil, salt, and black pepper to create a paste.
> Place the leg of lamb in a roasting pan, and using a sharp knife, make small incisions all over the lamb.
> Rub the herb and garlic paste over the entire surface of the lamb, ensuring it gets into the incisions.
> Roast the lamb in the preheated oven, allowing approximately 20 minutes of cooking time per pound for medium doneness. Use a meat thermometer to ensure the internal temperature reaches 145°F (63°C) for medium.
> Once done, remove the lamb from the oven and let it rest for 15-20 minutes before carving.

For the Mint Sauce:

> In a heatproof bowl, combine the finely chopped fresh mint leaves and sugar.
> Pour the boiling water over the mint and sugar mixture. Stir until the sugar is dissolved.
> Add the white wine vinegar to the mint mixture, stirring well.
> Allow the mint sauce to cool to room temperature before serving.

To Serve:

Carve the roast lamb into slices and serve with the mint sauce on the side. The refreshing mint sauce complements the rich flavors of the roast lamb perfectly. Enjoy your Roast Lamb with Mint Sauce as a delightful Easter or special occasion dish!

Deviled Eggs with Smoked Salmon

Ingredients:

- 6 hard-boiled eggs, peeled and halved
- 2 tablespoons mayonnaise
- 1 teaspoon Dijon mustard
- 1 teaspoon fresh lemon juice
- Salt and black pepper to taste
- 2 ounces smoked salmon, finely chopped
- Fresh dill, for garnish
- Capers, for garnish

Instructions:

Cut the hard-boiled eggs in half lengthwise, and carefully remove the yolks. Place the yolks in a bowl.

Mash the egg yolks with a fork, and add mayonnaise, Dijon mustard, fresh lemon juice, salt, and black pepper. Mix until smooth and well combined.

Gently fold in the finely chopped smoked salmon into the yolk mixture.

Spoon or pipe the smoked salmon and egg yolk mixture back into the egg white halves.

Garnish each deviled egg with a small piece of smoked salmon, a sprinkle of fresh dill, and a few capers.

Arrange the deviled eggs on a serving platter and refrigerate until ready to serve.

These Deviled Eggs with Smoked Salmon make a elegant and tasty appetizer for Easter or any special occasion. Enjoy!

Hot Cross Buns

Ingredients:

For the Buns:

- 4 cups all-purpose flour
- 1/2 cup sugar
- 1 packet (2 1/4 teaspoons) active dry yeast
- 1 1/2 teaspoons ground cinnamon
- 1/2 teaspoon ground nutmeg
- 1/2 teaspoon salt
- 1 1/4 cups warm milk (110°F/43°C)
- 1/4 cup unsalted butter, melted
- 1 large egg
- 1 cup currants or raisins

For the Cross:

- 1/2 cup all-purpose flour
- 1/2 cup water

For the Glaze:

- 1/4 cup apricot jam or preserves
- 1 tablespoon water

Instructions:

In a large bowl, combine 4 cups of flour, sugar, yeast, ground cinnamon, ground nutmeg, and salt.
In a separate bowl, whisk together warm milk, melted butter, and egg.
Pour the wet ingredients into the dry ingredients and mix until a soft dough forms.
Turn the dough out onto a floured surface and knead for about 8-10 minutes until it becomes smooth and elastic.
Knead in the currants or raisins during the last few minutes of kneading.
Place the dough in a greased bowl, cover it with a clean cloth, and let it rise in a warm place for 1-2 hours or until it has doubled in size.

Punch down the dough and divide it into 12 equal pieces. Shape each piece into a ball and place them in a greased 9x13-inch baking pan.

For the cross, mix 1/2 cup flour with 1/2 cup water to form a paste. Pipe or spoon a cross over the top of each bun.

Cover the buns with a clean cloth and let them rise for another 30-45 minutes.

Preheat your oven to 375°F (190°C).

Bake the buns in the preheated oven for 15-20 minutes or until golden brown.

While the buns are baking, prepare the glaze by heating apricot jam or preserves with 1 tablespoon of water in a small saucepan. Strain the glaze to remove any fruit pieces.

Once the buns are out of the oven, brush them with the apricot glaze while they are still warm.

Allow the buns to cool in the pan before serving.

These Hot Cross Buns are a classic Easter treat, and they're best enjoyed warm with a cup of tea. Enjoy!

Spinach and Feta Stuffed Mushrooms

Ingredients:

- 24 large white or cremini mushrooms, cleaned and stems removed
- 2 tablespoons olive oil
- 1 small onion, finely chopped
- 2 cloves garlic, minced
- 4 cups fresh spinach, chopped
- 1/2 cup crumbled feta cheese
- Salt and black pepper to taste
- 1/4 teaspoon red pepper flakes (optional)
- 2 tablespoons breadcrumbs (optional)
- Fresh parsley, chopped, for garnish

Instructions:

Preheat your oven to 375°F (190°C).
Clean the mushrooms and remove the stems. Place the mushroom caps on a baking sheet.
Finely chop the mushroom stems.
In a large skillet, heat olive oil over medium heat. Add chopped onion and cook until softened, about 3-4 minutes.
Add minced garlic to the skillet and cook for an additional 1-2 minutes until fragrant.
Add the chopped mushroom stems to the skillet and cook for 3-4 minutes until they release their moisture.
Stir in the chopped spinach and cook until wilted, about 2-3 minutes.
Remove the skillet from heat and let the mixture cool for a few minutes.
Once the mixture is slightly cooled, stir in the crumbled feta cheese. Season with salt, black pepper, and red pepper flakes (if using).
If the mixture seems too wet, you can add breadcrumbs to absorb excess moisture.
Fill each mushroom cap with a spoonful of the spinach and feta mixture, pressing it down slightly.
Bake the stuffed mushrooms in the preheated oven for 15-20 minutes or until the mushrooms are tender.
Garnish with fresh chopped parsley before serving.

These Spinach and Feta Stuffed Mushrooms make a delightful appetizer for any occasion, including Easter. Enjoy!

Lemon Herb Roasted Chicken

Ingredients:

- 1 whole roasting chicken (about 4-5 pounds)
- 1 lemon, sliced
- 4 cloves garlic, minced
- 2 tablespoons fresh rosemary, chopped
- 2 tablespoons fresh thyme, chopped
- 1/4 cup fresh parsley, chopped
- 1/4 cup olive oil
- Salt and black pepper to taste
- 1 cup chicken broth (or water) for roasting

Instructions:

Preheat your oven to 425°F (220°C).
Rinse the chicken inside and out, and pat it dry with paper towels.
In a small bowl, mix together minced garlic, chopped rosemary, chopped thyme, chopped parsley, olive oil, salt, and black pepper to create an herb paste.
Carefully loosen the skin from the chicken breast without completely detaching it. Rub the herb paste under the skin, massaging it over the breast meat.
Place lemon slices inside the chicken cavity.
Tie the legs together with kitchen twine and tuck the wing tips under the body of the chicken.
Place the chicken on a rack in a roasting pan, breast side up.
Pour chicken broth or water into the bottom of the roasting pan to prevent drippings from burning.
Roast the chicken in the preheated oven for about 15 minutes to allow the skin to brown.
Reduce the oven temperature to 375°F (190°C) and continue roasting for approximately 1 hour and 15 minutes, or until the internal temperature reaches 165°F (74°C) when measured at the thickest part of the thigh.
If the skin begins to brown too quickly, you can tent the chicken with aluminum foil.
Once done, remove the chicken from the oven and let it rest for about 15-20 minutes before carving.
Carve the lemon herb roasted chicken and serve with your favorite side dishes.

This Lemon Herb Roasted Chicken is a flavorful and classic choice for Easter or any special dinner. Enjoy!

Asparagus and Prosciutto Bundles

Ingredients:

- 1 pound fresh asparagus spears, trimmed
- 8 slices prosciutto
- 2 tablespoons olive oil
- 1 tablespoon balsamic glaze (optional)
- Salt and black pepper to taste
- Parmesan cheese, shaved, for garnish (optional)

Instructions:

Preheat your oven to 400°F (200°C).
Divide the trimmed asparagus into bundles, with about 5-6 spears per bundle.
Take a slice of prosciutto and wrap it around each bundle of asparagus, securing the ends.
Place the asparagus bundles on a baking sheet lined with parchment paper.
Drizzle the olive oil over the asparagus bundles and season with salt and black pepper.
Roast in the preheated oven for 12-15 minutes or until the asparagus is tender and the prosciutto is crispy.
If desired, drizzle balsamic glaze over the asparagus bundles before serving.
Optionally, garnish with shaved Parmesan cheese.
Serve the asparagus and prosciutto bundles as a side dish or appetizer.

These Asparagus and Prosciutto Bundles make an elegant and delicious addition to your Easter table or any special occasion. Enjoy!

Scalloped Potatoes

Ingredients:

- 2 1/2 pounds Yukon Gold potatoes, peeled and thinly sliced
- 1/4 cup unsalted butter
- 1/4 cup all-purpose flour
- 2 cups whole milk
- 1 cup heavy cream
- 2 cloves garlic, minced
- 1 teaspoon dried thyme
- Salt and black pepper to taste
- 2 cups shredded Gruyère or cheddar cheese
- 1/4 cup grated Parmesan cheese
- Fresh chives, chopped, for garnish (optional)

Instructions:

Preheat your oven to 375°F (190°C).
In a saucepan over medium heat, melt the butter. Add minced garlic and sauté until fragrant, about 1 minute.
Stir in the flour to create a roux. Cook for 2-3 minutes, whisking constantly to eliminate the raw flour taste.
Gradually whisk in the milk and heavy cream, continuing to whisk until the mixture thickens, usually around 5-7 minutes.
Add dried thyme, salt, and black pepper to the sauce, adjusting the seasoning to your taste.
Stir in 1 1/2 cups of shredded Gruyère or cheddar cheese until melted and the sauce is smooth. Reserve the remaining cheese for the top.
Layer half of the sliced potatoes in a greased 9x13-inch baking dish.
Pour half of the cheese sauce over the potatoes, spreading it evenly.
Repeat with the remaining sliced potatoes and cheese sauce.
In a small bowl, mix the remaining 1/2 cup of shredded cheese with grated Parmesan. Sprinkle this cheese mixture over the top.
Cover the baking dish with aluminum foil and bake in the preheated oven for 45 minutes.
Remove the foil and bake for an additional 15-20 minutes or until the potatoes are tender and the top is golden brown.

Let the scalloped potatoes rest for 10 minutes before serving. Garnish with chopped fresh chives if desired.

Serve these creamy and cheesy scalloped potatoes as a comforting and delicious side dish for your Easter dinner or any special meal. Enjoy!

Caprese Salad Skewers

Ingredients:

- Cherry tomatoes
- Fresh mozzarella balls (bocconcini)
- Fresh basil leaves
- Balsamic glaze
- Extra virgin olive oil
- Salt and black pepper to taste
- Wooden skewers

Instructions:

Start by assembling the skewers. Thread one cherry tomato, one mozzarella ball, and one basil leaf onto each wooden skewer. Repeat until you have the desired number of skewers.
Arrange the assembled skewers on a serving platter.
Drizzle balsamic glaze and extra virgin olive oil over the skewers.
Season with salt and black pepper to taste.
Optionally, you can sprinkle a bit more fresh basil over the top for added flavor and presentation.
Serve the Caprese Salad Skewers as a refreshing and bite-sized appetizer for your Easter gathering or any occasion.

These Caprese Salad Skewers capture the classic flavors of a Caprese salad in a convenient and delightful format. Enjoy!

Baked Salmon with Dill Sauce

Ingredients:

For the Baked Salmon:

- 4 salmon fillets
- 2 tablespoons olive oil
- 2 cloves garlic, minced
- 1 teaspoon lemon zest
- 1 tablespoon fresh lemon juice
- Salt and black pepper to taste
- Fresh dill, chopped, for garnish

For the Dill Sauce:

- 1/2 cup plain Greek yogurt
- 2 tablespoons mayonnaise
- 2 tablespoons fresh dill, chopped
- 1 tablespoon Dijon mustard
- 1 tablespoon fresh lemon juice
- Salt and black pepper to taste

Instructions:

For the Baked Salmon:

Preheat your oven to 375°F (190°C).
Place the salmon fillets on a baking sheet lined with parchment paper.
In a small bowl, mix together olive oil, minced garlic, lemon zest, and lemon juice.
Brush the salmon fillets with the olive oil mixture, coating them evenly. Season with salt and black pepper.
Bake the salmon in the preheated oven for 12-15 minutes or until the fish flakes easily with a fork.
Remove the salmon from the oven and garnish with chopped fresh dill.

For the Dill Sauce:

In a bowl, whisk together Greek yogurt, mayonnaise, chopped dill, Dijon mustard, and fresh lemon juice.

Season the dill sauce with salt and black pepper to taste.

Serve the baked salmon fillets with a dollop of dill sauce on top.

Garnish with additional chopped dill for a burst of freshness.

This Baked Salmon with Dill Sauce is a flavorful and healthy option for your Easter dinner or any special occasion. Enjoy!

Carrot Ginger Soup

Ingredients:

- 1 tablespoon olive oil
- 1 onion, chopped
- 2 pounds carrots, peeled and chopped
- 2 tablespoons fresh ginger, grated
- 3 cloves garlic, minced
- 4 cups vegetable broth
- 1 cup coconut milk
- Salt and black pepper to taste
- 1 tablespoon honey (optional, for sweetness)
- Fresh cilantro or parsley, chopped, for garnish (optional)

Instructions:

In a large pot, heat olive oil over medium heat. Add chopped onions and sauté until they become translucent, about 5 minutes.

Add chopped carrots, grated ginger, and minced garlic to the pot. Continue to sauté for another 5 minutes.

Pour in the vegetable broth, ensuring that the carrots are mostly covered. Bring the mixture to a boil, then reduce the heat to simmer. Cover the pot and let it cook until the carrots are tender, approximately 15-20 minutes.

Use an immersion blender to puree the soup until smooth. If you don't have an immersion blender, carefully transfer the soup in batches to a blender and blend until smooth. Be cautious, as hot liquids can expand in a blender.

Return the pureed soup to the pot. Stir in coconut milk and season with salt and black pepper to taste. If you prefer a sweeter taste, add honey and adjust according to your preference.

Continue to heat the soup over low heat for an additional 5 minutes, allowing the flavors to meld.

Serve the Carrot Ginger Soup hot, garnished with fresh cilantro or parsley if desired.

This Carrot Ginger Soup is not only delicious but also rich in nutrients, making it a comforting and healthy choice for your Easter or any time you crave a warm bowl of soup. Enjoy!

Pesto Deviled Eggs

Ingredients:

- 6 hard-boiled eggs, peeled and halved
- 3 tablespoons mayonnaise
- 2 tablespoons pesto sauce (store-bought or homemade)
- 1 teaspoon Dijon mustard
- Salt and black pepper to taste
- Fresh basil leaves, for garnish (optional)
- Pine nuts, toasted, for garnish (optional)

Instructions:

Cut the hard-boiled eggs in half lengthwise, and carefully remove the yolks. Place the yolks in a bowl.
Mash the egg yolks with a fork, and add mayonnaise, pesto sauce, Dijon mustard, salt, and black pepper. Mix until smooth and well combined.
Spoon or pipe the pesto deviled egg mixture back into the egg white halves.
Optionally, garnish each deviled egg with a small basil leaf and a sprinkle of toasted pine nuts.
Arrange the Pesto Deviled Eggs on a serving platter.
Refrigerate until ready to serve.

These Pesto Deviled Eggs add a flavorful and vibrant twist to the classic recipe, making them a delightful appetizer for Easter or any occasion. Enjoy!

Garlic Rosemary Roasted Lamb

Ingredients:

- 1 leg of lamb (5-7 pounds)
- 6 cloves garlic, minced
- 2 tablespoons fresh rosemary, chopped
- 3 tablespoons olive oil
- 1 tablespoon Dijon mustard
- 1 tablespoon balsamic vinegar
- Salt and black pepper to taste
- 1 cup red wine (optional)
- 1 cup beef or vegetable broth

Instructions:

Preheat your oven to 375°F (190°C).
In a small bowl, mix minced garlic, chopped rosemary, olive oil, Dijon mustard, balsamic vinegar, salt, and black pepper to create a marinade.
Place the leg of lamb in a roasting pan, fat side up.
Rub the marinade over the entire surface of the lamb, ensuring it's evenly coated.
Optionally, pour red wine into the bottom of the roasting pan for added flavor.
Add beef or vegetable broth to the pan to prevent drippings from burning.
Roast the lamb in the preheated oven for approximately 20 minutes per pound for medium doneness. Use a meat thermometer to ensure the internal temperature reaches 145°F (63°C) for medium.
Baste the lamb with pan juices every 30 minutes to keep it moist and flavorful.
Once done, remove the lamb from the oven and let it rest for 15-20 minutes before carving.
Strain the pan juices for a delicious gravy to serve alongside the lamb.
Carve the garlic rosemary roasted lamb and serve with the pan juices or your preferred gravy.

This Garlic Rosemary Roasted Lamb is a classic and savory choice for a festive meal, making it perfect for Easter or any special occasion. Enjoy!

Spring Pea Risotto

Ingredients:

- 1 1/2 cups Arborio rice
- 1 cup fresh or frozen peas
- 1 small onion, finely chopped
- 2 cloves garlic, minced
- 4 cups vegetable broth, kept warm
- 1/2 cup dry white wine
- 1/2 cup Parmesan cheese, grated
- 2 tablespoons unsalted butter
- 2 tablespoons olive oil
- Salt and black pepper to taste
- Fresh mint or basil, chopped, for garnish
- Lemon zest, for garnish (optional)

Instructions:

In a saucepan, heat the vegetable broth over low heat and keep it warm.
In a large, deep skillet or a wide saucepan, heat olive oil over medium heat. Add chopped onions and sauté until they become translucent.
Add minced garlic to the skillet and cook for an additional 1-2 minutes until fragrant.
Add Arborio rice to the skillet, stirring to coat the rice in the oil and onions. Toast the rice for 1-2 minutes until it becomes slightly translucent around the edges.
Pour in the white wine, stirring continuously until the wine is absorbed by the rice.
Begin adding the warm vegetable broth one ladle at a time, allowing the liquid to be absorbed before adding the next ladle. Stir the rice frequently.
Continue this process until the rice is creamy and cooked to al dente, which should take about 18-20 minutes.
In the last 5 minutes of cooking, add fresh or frozen peas to the risotto, allowing them to cook through.
Once the risotto is cooked, stir in Parmesan cheese and butter. Season with salt and black pepper to taste.
Remove the risotto from heat, and let it rest for a minute.
Serve the Spring Pea Risotto hot, garnished with chopped fresh mint or basil. Optionally, sprinkle some lemon zest over the top for a burst of freshness.

Enjoy this creamy and vibrant Spring Pea Risotto as a delightful side dish for your Easter celebration or any special occasion!

Shrimp Cocktail

Ingredients:

For the Shrimp:

- 1 pound large shrimp, peeled and deveined
- 1 lemon, sliced
- 1 bay leaf
- 1 teaspoon black peppercorns
- Salt, to taste
- Ice, for serving

For the Cocktail Sauce:

- 1 cup ketchup
- 2 tablespoons horseradish (adjust to taste)
- 1 tablespoon Worcestershire sauce
- 1 tablespoon fresh lemon juice
- Hot sauce, to taste (optional)
- Salt and black pepper, to taste

For Garnish:

- Fresh parsley, chopped
- Lemon wedges

Instructions:

For the Shrimp:

Fill a large pot with water and add lemon slices, bay leaf, black peppercorns, and salt. Bring the water to a boil.
Add the shrimp to the boiling water and cook for 2-3 minutes or until the shrimp turn pink and opaque.
Drain the shrimp and immediately transfer them to a bowl of ice water to stop the cooking process.

Once the shrimp are cooled, drain them and refrigerate until ready to serve.

For the Cocktail Sauce:

In a bowl, mix together ketchup, horseradish, Worcestershire sauce, fresh lemon juice, and hot sauce (if using).
Season the cocktail sauce with salt and black pepper to taste. Adjust the horseradish and hot sauce according to your desired level of heat.

To Serve:

Arrange the chilled shrimp on a serving platter or individual cocktail glasses over a bed of ice.
Place a bowl of cocktail sauce in the center or alongside the shrimp.
Garnish with chopped fresh parsley and lemon wedges.
Serve the Shrimp Cocktail immediately, allowing guests to dip the shrimp into the cocktail sauce.

This classic Shrimp Cocktail is a refreshing and elegant appetizer, perfect for any occasion, including Easter. Enjoy!

Raspberry Almond Tart

Ingredients:

For the Tart Crust:

- 1 1/4 cups all-purpose flour
- 1/2 cup unsalted butter, cold and cubed
- 1/4 cup granulated sugar
- 1 large egg yolk
- 2 tablespoons ice water

For the Almond Filling:

- 1 cup almond flour
- 1/2 cup granulated sugar
- 1/4 cup unsalted butter, softened
- 1 large egg
- 1 teaspoon almond extract

For Topping:

- 1 cup fresh raspberries
- Powdered sugar, for dusting

Instructions:

For the Tart Crust:

In a food processor, combine the flour, cold cubed butter, and sugar. Pulse until the mixture resembles coarse crumbs.
Add the egg yolk and pulse again.
With the food processor running, add ice water gradually until the dough comes together.
Turn the dough out onto a floured surface and knead it lightly. Shape the dough into a disk, wrap it in plastic wrap, and refrigerate for at least 30 minutes.
Preheat your oven to 375°F (190°C).

Roll out the chilled dough on a floured surface and fit it into a tart pan. Press the dough into the edges and trim any excess.

Line the tart crust with parchment paper and fill it with pie weights or dried beans.

Bake the tart crust in the preheated oven for 15 minutes. Remove the weights and parchment paper, then bake for an additional 5-7 minutes or until the crust is golden brown. Let it cool.

For the Almond Filling:

In a bowl, combine almond flour, sugar, softened butter, egg, and almond extract. Mix until smooth.

Assembly:

Spread the almond filling evenly over the cooled tart crust.

Arrange fresh raspberries on top of the almond filling.

Bake the tart in the oven for about 20-25 minutes or until the almond filling is set and golden brown.

Let the Raspberry Almond Tart cool completely.

Dust the tart with powdered sugar just before serving.

Slice and enjoy this delightful Raspberry Almond Tart as a sweet treat for Easter or any special occasion.

This tart combines the nutty richness of almond filling with the vibrant sweetness of fresh raspberries, creating a beautiful and delicious dessert. Enjoy!

Easter Bunny Cupcakes

Ingredients:

For the Cupcakes:

- 1 box of your favorite cupcake mix (plus required ingredients)

For the Buttercream Frosting:

- 1 cup unsalted butter, softened
- 4 cups powdered sugar
- 1/4 cup whole milk or heavy cream
- 1 teaspoon vanilla extract
- Pink food coloring

For Decorating:

- Mini marshmallows
- Pink jelly beans or small candies (for noses)
- Black gel icing or small chocolate chips (for eyes)
- Shredded coconut (optional, for fur)
- Pink or white candy melts (for bunny ears)

Instructions:

For the Cupcakes:

Preheat your oven according to the cupcake mix instructions.
Prepare the cupcake batter as directed on the box.
Line a cupcake pan with cupcake liners and fill each cupcake liner about 2/3 full with batter.
Bake the cupcakes according to the package instructions. Allow them to cool completely before frosting.

For the Buttercream Frosting:

In a large mixing bowl, beat the softened butter until creamy.
Gradually add powdered sugar, alternating with milk or cream, and continue to beat until smooth and fluffy.
Mix in the vanilla extract.
Add pink food coloring to achieve the desired shade for the bunny ears.

For Decorating:

Once the cupcakes are completely cooled, frost them with the pink buttercream.
For the bunny ears, melt pink or white candy melts and pipe two large bunny ears onto parchment paper. Allow them to set.
Attach the bunny ears to the top of each cupcake.
Use mini marshmallows to create the cheeks of the bunny by placing two on each cupcake.
Add a pink jelly bean or small candy for the bunny nose.
Use black gel icing or small chocolate chips to create eyes.
If desired, you can use shredded coconut to create a fur-like texture around the bunny's face.
Serve and enjoy these adorable Easter Bunny Cupcakes!

These Easter Bunny Cupcakes are not only cute but also a delicious addition to your Easter celebration. Enjoy the festive sweetness!

Grilled Vegetable Platter

Ingredients:

Assorted vegetables (choose a variety of colors and types):

- Bell peppers (red, yellow, green)
- Zucchini
- Eggplant
- Cherry tomatoes
- Red onions
- Mushrooms
- Asparagus

Marinade:

- 1/4 cup olive oil
- 2 cloves garlic, minced
- 2 tablespoons balsamic vinegar
- 1 teaspoon dried oregano
- Salt and pepper to taste

Instructions:

Preheat your grill to medium-high heat.
Wash and prepare the vegetables. Cut the bell peppers into thick strips, slice the zucchini and eggplant into rounds, halve the cherry tomatoes, and trim the asparagus.
In a small bowl, whisk together the olive oil, minced garlic, balsamic vinegar, dried oregano, salt, and pepper to create the marinade.
Place the prepared vegetables in a large bowl and pour the marinade over them. Toss the vegetables until they are evenly coated with the marinade.
Thread the vegetables onto skewers or place them directly on the grill grates.
Grill the vegetables for about 8-10 minutes, turning occasionally, until they are tender and have nice grill marks.
Arrange the grilled vegetables on a serving platter.

Optional: Drizzle a little extra balsamic vinegar or olive oil over the grilled vegetables for added flavor.

Serve the grilled vegetable platter as a side dish, appetizer, or even as a main course. It's a versatile and colorful dish that complements many meals.

Feel free to customize the recipe based on your preferences, and enjoy this healthy and tasty Grilled Vegetable Platter!

Apricot Glazed Roast Chicken

Ingredients:

- 1 whole chicken (about 4-5 pounds)
- Salt and black pepper to taste
- 1 teaspoon garlic powder
- 1 teaspoon onion powder
- 1 teaspoon dried thyme
- 1 teaspoon paprika
- 1/2 cup apricot preserves
- 2 tablespoons Dijon mustard
- 2 tablespoons soy sauce
- 2 tablespoons olive oil
- 1 tablespoon apple cider vinegar
- 2 cloves garlic, minced
- Fresh parsley, chopped (for garnish)

Instructions:

Preheat your oven to 375°F (190°C).

Rinse the chicken under cold water and pat it dry with paper towels. Season the chicken, both inside and out, with salt, black pepper, garlic powder, onion powder, dried thyme, and paprika.

In a small saucepan over medium heat, combine apricot preserves, Dijon mustard, soy sauce, olive oil, apple cider vinegar, and minced garlic. Stir well and cook for a few minutes until the mixture is well combined and slightly thickened. Set aside.

Place the seasoned chicken on a roasting pan or in a baking dish.

Brush the apricot glaze generously over the entire surface of the chicken, using a basting brush.

Roast the chicken in the preheated oven for about 1 hour and 15 minutes or until the internal temperature reaches 165°F (74°C), basting with the apricot glaze every 20-30 minutes.

Once the chicken is cooked through, remove it from the oven and let it rest for about 10 minutes before carving.

Garnish the apricot glazed roast chicken with chopped fresh parsley before serving.

Serve the succulent apricot glazed roast chicken with your favorite side dishes, such as roasted vegetables, rice, or a salad.

This recipe creates a perfect balance of sweet and savory flavors, making it a delicious and impressive dish for a special dinner or family gathering. Enjoy!

Bacon-Wrapped Asparagus

Ingredients:

- Fresh asparagus spears, woody ends trimmed
- Thin-cut bacon strips
- Olive oil
- Black pepper
- Optional: Grated Parmesan cheese for garnish

Instructions:

Preheat your oven to 400°F (200°C).
Take a bundle of asparagus spears (about 4-5 spears) and wrap a slice of bacon around them. Repeat until all the asparagus spears are wrapped in bacon.
Place the bacon-wrapped asparagus bundles on a baking sheet lined with parchment paper or aluminum foil, seam side down, to prevent the bacon from unraveling.
Brush or drizzle olive oil over the bacon-wrapped asparagus to help with browning and add extra flavor. Sprinkle black pepper on top.
Bake in the preheated oven for 20-25 minutes or until the bacon is crispy and the asparagus is tender. You can also broil for a few minutes at the end to make the bacon extra crispy.
Optional: Sprinkle grated Parmesan cheese over the bacon-wrapped asparagus during the last few minutes of baking or broiling for a cheesy finish.
Remove from the oven and let the bacon-wrapped asparagus cool for a few minutes.
Serve the bacon-wrapped asparagus as an appetizer or a side dish. They make a great addition to brunch, parties, or as a tasty snack.

Feel free to customize this recipe by adding your favorite seasonings or herbs. The combination of smoky bacon and fresh asparagus is sure to be a crowd-pleaser. Enjoy!

Lemon Blueberry Cheesecake

Ingredients:

For the Crust:

- 1 1/2 cups graham cracker crumbs
- 1/3 cup unsalted butter, melted
- 2 tablespoons granulated sugar

For the Cheesecake Filling:

- 4 packages (32 ounces) cream cheese, softened
- 1 1/4 cups granulated sugar
- 1 teaspoon vanilla extract
- Zest of 2 lemons
- 3 tablespoons lemon juice
- 4 large eggs
- 1 cup sour cream
- 1 cup fresh blueberries (tossed in 1 tablespoon of flour to prevent sinking)

For the Blueberry Sauce:

- 1 cup fresh or frozen blueberries
- 1/4 cup granulated sugar
- 2 tablespoons lemon juice
- 1 teaspoon cornstarch dissolved in 1 tablespoon water

Additional Toppings (optional):

- Whipped cream
- Lemon zest
- Fresh blueberries

Instructions:

For the Crust:

>Preheat your oven to 325°F (163°C). Grease a 9-inch springform pan.
>In a bowl, mix graham cracker crumbs, melted butter, and sugar until well combined.

Press the mixture into the bottom of the prepared springform pan, creating an even crust.

Bake the crust for 10 minutes. Remove from the oven and let it cool while preparing the filling.

For the Cheesecake Filling:

In a large mixing bowl, beat the softened cream cheese until smooth.

Add sugar, vanilla extract, lemon zest, and lemon juice. Mix until well combined.

Add eggs, one at a time, mixing well after each addition.

Fold in sour cream until smooth.

Gently fold in the blueberries coated in flour to prevent sinking.

Pour the cheesecake filling over the crust in the springform pan.

Bake in the preheated oven for about 1 hour or until the center is set and the edges are lightly golden.

Turn off the oven and leave the cheesecake inside for an additional hour to cool gradually.

Refrigerate the cheesecake for at least 4 hours or overnight before removing it from the springform pan.

For the Blueberry Sauce:

In a saucepan, combine blueberries, sugar, and lemon juice. Cook over medium heat until the blueberries burst and release their juices.

Stir in the cornstarch mixture and continue to cook until the sauce thickens.

Remove from heat and let it cool.

Assembly:

Once the cheesecake is thoroughly chilled, carefully remove it from the springform pan.

Pour the blueberry sauce over the top of the cheesecake.

Optional: Garnish with whipped cream, lemon zest, and additional fresh blueberries.

Slice and serve your delicious Lemon Blueberry Cheesecake!

Enjoy this delightful and refreshing dessert!

Greek Salad

Ingredients:

For the Salad:

- 4 cups cherry tomatoes, halved
- 1 cucumber, diced
- 1 red onion, thinly sliced
- 1 bell pepper (red, yellow, or green), diced
- 1 cup Kalamata olives, pitted
- 1 cup feta cheese, crumbled
- 1 cup cucumber, diced
- 1 cup red onion, thinly sliced
- 1 cup bell pepper (red, yellow, or green), diced
- 1 cup Kalamata olives, pitted
- 1 cup feta cheese, crumbled

For the Dressing:

- 1/3 cup extra-virgin olive oil
- 3 tablespoons red wine vinegar
- 1 teaspoon dried oregano
- 1 clove garlic, minced
- Salt and pepper to taste

Instructions:

In a large salad bowl, combine the cherry tomatoes, cucumber, red onion, bell pepper, olives, and feta cheese.
In a small bowl or jar, whisk together the olive oil, red wine vinegar, dried oregano, minced garlic, salt, and pepper. Adjust the seasoning to taste.
Pour the dressing over the salad and toss gently to coat all the ingredients evenly.
Let the Greek salad sit for a few minutes to allow the flavors to meld.
Serve the Greek salad immediately as a refreshing side dish or as a light and healthy main course.
Optionally, garnish with additional crumbled feta, a sprinkle of dried oregano, and a few Kalamata olives on top.

This Greek Salad is perfect for summer or any time you crave a light, vibrant, and satisfying dish. It pairs well with grilled meats, fish, or can be enjoyed on its own. Enjoy your delicious and nutritious Greek Salad!

Raspberry Lemon Muffins

Ingredients:

Dry Ingredients:

- 2 cups all-purpose flour
- 1/2 cup granulated sugar
- 1 tablespoon baking powder
- 1/2 teaspoon baking soda
- 1/4 teaspoon salt

Wet Ingredients:

- 1 cup buttermilk
- 1/2 cup unsalted butter, melted and cooled
- 2 large eggs
- Zest of 2 lemons
- 2 tablespoons fresh lemon juice
- 1 teaspoon vanilla extract

Additional Ingredients:

- 1 1/2 cups fresh raspberries
- 1 tablespoon all-purpose flour (for coating raspberries)

Instructions:

Preheat your oven to 375°F (190°C). Line a muffin tin with paper liners or grease the muffin cups.

In a small bowl, toss the fresh raspberries with 1 tablespoon of flour to coat them lightly. This helps prevent the raspberries from sinking to the bottom of the muffins.

In a large mixing bowl, whisk together the flour, sugar, baking powder, baking soda, and salt.

In another bowl, whisk together the buttermilk, melted butter, eggs, lemon zest, lemon juice, and vanilla extract until well combined.

Pour the wet ingredients into the dry ingredients and gently stir until just combined. Do not overmix; it's okay if there are a few lumps.

Carefully fold in the flour-coated raspberries into the batter.

Spoon the batter into the prepared muffin cups, filling each about 2/3 full.

Optional: Sprinkle a little extra sugar on top of each muffin for a slightly crunchy top.
Bake in the preheated oven for 18-20 minutes or until a toothpick inserted into the center comes out clean.
Allow the muffins to cool in the tin for 5 minutes before transferring them to a wire rack to cool completely.
Once cooled, you can optionally drizzle the tops with a simple lemon glaze made by mixing powdered sugar with lemon juice until you reach your desired consistency.
Serve and enjoy your Raspberry Lemon Muffins!

These muffins are perfect for breakfast, brunch, or as a sweet treat any time of the day.

The combination of tart raspberries and citrusy lemon creates a delightful and refreshing flavor profile.

Stuffed Bell Peppers with Quinoa

Ingredients:

For the Stuffed Bell Peppers:

- 4 large bell peppers (any color)
- 1 cup quinoa, rinsed and cooked according to package instructions
- 1 can (15 oz) black beans, drained and rinsed
- 1 cup corn kernels (fresh or frozen)
- 1 cup cherry tomatoes, diced
- 1 cup red onion, finely chopped
- 1 cup shredded cheddar or Mexican blend cheese
- 2 cloves garlic, minced
- 1 teaspoon ground cumin
- 1 teaspoon chili powder
- Salt and pepper to taste
- Olive oil for cooking

For the Sauce:

- 1 can (15 oz) tomato sauce
- 1 teaspoon dried oregano
- 1 teaspoon dried basil
- Salt and pepper to taste

Instructions:

Preparing the Quinoa and Filling:

> Preheat the oven to 375°F (190°C).
> Cook the quinoa according to package instructions. Set aside.
> In a large skillet, heat olive oil over medium heat. Add minced garlic and cook until fragrant.
> Add chopped red onion and cook until softened.
> Stir in black beans, corn, cherry tomatoes, cooked quinoa, ground cumin, chili powder, salt, and pepper. Cook for an additional 3-4 minutes until the mixture is well combined and heated through.
> Remove the skillet from heat and let the filling cool slightly.

Preparing the Bell Peppers:

Cut the tops off the bell peppers and remove the seeds and membranes. Lightly brush the outside of the peppers with olive oil.

Place the bell peppers in a baking dish, standing upright.

Fill each bell pepper with the quinoa and vegetable mixture, pressing it down gently.

Making the Sauce:

In a bowl, mix together the tomato sauce, dried oregano, dried basil, salt, and pepper.

Pour the tomato sauce mixture over the stuffed bell peppers.

Baking:

Cover the baking dish with aluminum foil and bake in the preheated oven for about 25-30 minutes.

Remove the foil and sprinkle shredded cheese over each stuffed bell pepper.

Bake for an additional 10-15 minutes or until the cheese is melted and bubbly, and the peppers are tender.

Remove from the oven and let them cool for a few minutes before serving.

Garnish with fresh herbs like cilantro or parsley if desired.

Serve the Stuffed Bell Peppers with Quinoa warm and enjoy!

These stuffed bell peppers make a wholesome and satisfying meal, packed with protein and a variety of vegetables. They're not only delicious but also a colorful addition to your dinner table.

Chocolate Covered Strawberries

Ingredients:

- Fresh strawberries, washed and dried
- Dark, milk, or white chocolate (about 8 ounces)
- Optional: White chocolate, melted (for drizzling)
- Optional toppings: Chopped nuts, shredded coconut, sprinkles

Instructions:

Prepare the Strawberries:
- Make sure the strawberries are completely dry. Any moisture can cause the chocolate to seize.
- Line a baking sheet with parchment paper to place the dipped strawberries.

Melt the Chocolate:
- Chop the chocolate into small, uniform pieces for even melting.
- In a heatproof bowl, melt the chocolate using a double boiler or in the microwave in short 20-30 second bursts, stirring between each burst. Be careful not to overheat, as chocolate can easily burn.

Dip the Strawberries:
- Hold each strawberry by the stem and dip it into the melted chocolate, making sure to coat about two-thirds of the berry.
- Allow excess chocolate to drip off or gently shake the strawberry.

Optional: Add Toppings:
- If desired, immediately roll the chocolate-covered strawberry in chopped nuts, shredded coconut, or sprinkles while the chocolate is still wet.

Place on Parchment Paper:
- Place the dipped strawberries on the prepared parchment paper-lined baking sheet.

Allow to Set:
- Let the chocolate-covered strawberries cool and set at room temperature. You can also place them in the refrigerator for quicker setting.

Optional: Drizzle with White Chocolate:
- If you'd like, melt a small amount of white chocolate and drizzle it over the dipped strawberries using a spoon or a piping bag for a decorative touch.

Serve and Enjoy:
- Once the chocolate is fully set, serve the chocolate-covered strawberries on a platter or in cupcake liners.

Storage:
- Store any leftover chocolate-covered strawberries in the refrigerator. They are best enjoyed within 24-48 hours for optimal freshness.

Chocolate Covered Strawberries are a delightful treat for special occasions, celebrations, or just a sweet indulgence. Customize them with your favorite toppings and enjoy the perfect combination of juicy strawberries and rich, smooth chocolate!

Roasted Vegetable Quiche

Ingredients:

For the Roasted Vegetables:

- 2 cups mixed vegetables, diced (such as bell peppers, zucchini, cherry tomatoes, red onion, mushrooms)
- 2 tablespoons olive oil
- Salt and pepper to taste
- 1 teaspoon dried herbs (such as thyme, rosemary, or oregano)

For the Quiche Filling:

- 1 pre-made pie crust (store-bought or homemade)
- 1 cup shredded cheese (cheddar, Swiss, or your choice)
- 1 cup milk (whole or 2%)
- 4 large eggs
- Salt and pepper to taste
- 1/2 teaspoon garlic powder
- 1/2 teaspoon dried herbs (thyme, rosemary, or oregano)
- Optional: 1/4 cup grated Parmesan cheese

Instructions:

For the Roasted Vegetables:

Preheat the oven to 400°F (200°C).
In a large bowl, toss the diced vegetables with olive oil, salt, pepper, and dried herbs.
Spread the vegetables on a baking sheet lined with parchment paper.
Roast the vegetables in the preheated oven for 20-25 minutes or until they are tender and slightly caramelized. Stir occasionally for even roasting.
Remove the vegetables from the oven and set aside.

For the Quiche Filling:

Preheat the oven to 375°F (190°C).
Roll out the pie crust and fit it into a pie dish. Crimp the edges for a decorative finish.
In a mixing bowl, whisk together the eggs, milk, salt, pepper, garlic powder, and dried herbs until well combined.
Sprinkle the shredded cheese over the bottom of the pie crust.
Spread the roasted vegetables evenly over the cheese.

Pour the egg mixture over the vegetables and cheese.
Optional: Sprinkle grated Parmesan cheese on top for extra flavor.
Bake in the preheated oven for 30-35 minutes or until the quiche is set and the top is golden brown.
Allow the quiche to cool for a few minutes before slicing.

Serving:

Slice the roasted vegetable quiche into wedges.
Serve warm or at room temperature.

This Roasted Vegetable Quiche is perfect for brunch, lunch, or a light dinner. Feel free to customize the vegetables and cheese based on your preferences. Enjoy the delicious combination of roasted veggies and a flavorful egg filling!

Easter Nest Cookies

Ingredients:

- 1 cup unsalted butter, softened
- 1 cup granulated sugar
- 2 large eggs
- 1 teaspoon vanilla extract
- 2 cups all-purpose flour
- 1/2 teaspoon baking powder
- 1/4 teaspoon salt
- 2 cups sweetened shredded coconut
- Mini chocolate eggs or jelly beans for decorating

Instructions:

Preheat the oven: Preheat your oven to 350°F (175°C) and line a baking sheet with parchment paper.
Cream the butter and sugar: In a large mixing bowl, cream together the softened butter and granulated sugar until light and fluffy.
Add eggs and vanilla: Beat in the eggs one at a time, then add the vanilla extract and mix well.
Combine dry ingredients: In a separate bowl, whisk together the flour, baking powder, and salt. Gradually add this dry mixture to the wet ingredients, mixing until just combined.
Form cookie nests: Scoop out tablespoon-sized portions of dough and shape them into nests on the prepared baking sheet. Use your fingers or the back of a spoon to create an indentation in the center of each nest.
Add coconut: Sprinkle sweetened shredded coconut around the edges of each nest, pressing it gently into the dough.
Bake: Bake in the preheated oven for 10-12 minutes or until the edges are golden brown. Keep an eye on them to avoid over-baking.
Decorate: Once out of the oven, immediately press mini chocolate eggs or jelly beans into the center of each nest, creating the "eggs" in the nest.
Cool: Allow the cookies to cool on the baking sheet for a few minutes before transferring them to a wire rack to cool completely.
Serve and enjoy: Once completely cooled, your Easter Nest Cookies are ready to be enjoyed. They make a charming addition to any Easter celebration!

Feel free to get creative with the decorations, using pastel-colored candies or other Easter-themed treats to make these cookies even more festive.

Broccoli and Cheddar Casserole

Ingredients:

- 4 cups fresh broccoli florets
- 1/4 cup unsalted butter
- 1/4 cup all-purpose flour
- 1/2 teaspoon salt
- 1/4 teaspoon black pepper
- 2 cups whole milk
- 2 cups shredded sharp cheddar cheese
- 1 cup breadcrumbs
- 2 tablespoons melted butter for topping

Instructions:

Preheat the Oven: Preheat your oven to 350°F (175°C). Grease a baking dish (9x13 inches or a similar size).

Blanch the Broccoli: Bring a large pot of salted water to a boil. Add the broccoli florets and cook for 2-3 minutes, or until they are bright green and slightly tender. Drain and set aside.

Make the Cheese Sauce: In a medium saucepan, melt 1/4 cup of butter over medium heat. Stir in the flour, salt, and pepper until well combined to make a roux. Gradually whisk in the milk, stirring constantly to avoid lumps. Cook until the mixture thickens, usually about 5 minutes.

Add Cheese: Remove the saucepan from heat and stir in the shredded cheddar cheese until smooth and fully melted.

Combine with Broccoli: Place the blanched broccoli in the prepared baking dish. Pour the cheese sauce over the broccoli, making sure it is evenly distributed.

Top with Breadcrumbs: In a small bowl, mix the breadcrumbs with melted butter. Sprinkle the breadcrumb mixture evenly over the broccoli and cheese.

Bake: Bake in the preheated oven for 25-30 minutes, or until the casserole is bubbly, and the breadcrumbs are golden brown.

Serve: Allow the casserole to cool for a few minutes before serving. Enjoy your delicious and cheesy Broccoli and Cheddar Casserole!

Feel free to customize the recipe by adding other ingredients like diced ham or cooked chicken for a heartier version. This casserole makes for a tasty side dish or a satisfying main course.

Mint Chocolate Chip Ice Cream Cake

Ingredients:

For the Cake Base:

- 2 cups chocolate cookie crumbs (you can use chocolate graham crackers or chocolate sandwich cookies)
- 1/2 cup unsalted butter, melted

For the Ice Cream Layers:

- 1.5 quarts mint chocolate chip ice cream, softened

For the Chocolate Ganache:

- 1 cup semi-sweet chocolate chips
- 1/2 cup heavy cream

For Garnish (Optional):

- Crushed mint candies or chocolate shavings

Instructions:

1. Prepare the Cake Base:

- In a bowl, mix the chocolate cookie crumbs with melted butter until well combined.
- Press the mixture into the bottom of a springform pan or a lined cake pan to create an even crust.
- Place the crust in the freezer to set while you prepare the ice cream.

2. Layer the Ice Cream:

- Once the cake base is firm, spread a layer of softened mint chocolate chip ice cream over the crust.
- Place the pan back in the freezer to let the ice cream layer freeze and set for about 30 minutes to an hour.
- Repeat the process with another layer of mint chocolate chip ice cream.

3. Prepare the Chocolate Ganache:

- In a heatproof bowl, combine the chocolate chips and heavy cream.
- Microwave in 30-second intervals, stirring in between, until the chocolate is fully melted and the mixture is smooth.
- Let the ganache cool slightly.

4. Final Assembly:

- Pour the chocolate ganache over the top of the ice cream layers, spreading it evenly.
- If desired, garnish with crushed mint candies or chocolate shavings for an extra touch.
- Place the cake back in the freezer to set for at least 4-6 hours or overnight.

5. Serving:

- Before serving, let the ice cream cake sit at room temperature for a few minutes to make it easier to slice.
- Use a sharp knife dipped in warm water to cut clean slices.

Enjoy your delicious Mint Chocolate Chip Ice Cream Cake! This dessert is perfect for celebrations or as a refreshing treat during warmer months.

Smoked Salmon Platter

Ingredients:

1. Smoked Salmon:

    - 8-12 ounces of high-quality smoked salmon slices

2. Bagels or Bread:

    - Sliced bagels or your choice of bread (rye, pumpernickel, or whole grain work well)

3. Cream Cheese:

    - 1 cup of cream cheese, softened
    - Optional: flavored cream cheese (such as chive or dill)

4. Fresh Vegetables:

    - Red onion, thinly sliced
    - Cucumber, thinly sliced
    - Tomatoes, sliced

5. Capers:

    - 1/4 cup capers, drained

6. Lemon:

    - Lemon wedges for squeezing over the salmon

7. Fresh Herbs:

    - Fresh dill, chopped, for garnish

8. Additional Garnishes (Optional):

- Radishes, avocado slices, pickles, or microgreens

Instructions:

1. Arrange the Smoked Salmon:

- Lay the smoked salmon slices on a serving platter. You can slightly overlap them for an attractive presentation.

2. Prepare the Cream Cheese:

- If you're using plain cream cheese, you can either spread it on the bagels or present it in a separate bowl. If using flavored cream cheese, spread it onto the bagels.

3. Slice and Arrange the Bagels or Bread:

- Slice the bagels or bread and arrange them on the platter or on a separate plate.

4. Add Fresh Vegetables:

- Arrange the sliced red onion, cucumber, and tomatoes around the smoked salmon.

5. Garnish with Capers:

- Sprinkle capers over the smoked salmon for a burst of briny flavor.

6. Lemon Wedges:

- Place lemon wedges on the platter for guests to squeeze over their salmon.

7. Fresh Herbs and Additional Garnishes:

- Sprinkle chopped fresh dill over the salmon for a touch of freshness. Add any extra garnishes like radishes, avocado slices, pickles, or microgreens if desired.

8. Serve:

- Serve the smoked salmon platter immediately. You can also include additional condiments like mustard, horseradish, or a honey-mustard sauce on the side.

This Smoked Salmon Platter is not only visually appealing but also offers a variety of flavors and textures. It's a fantastic way to showcase the delicate taste of smoked salmon and create a memorable dining experience for your guests.

Spring Pea and Mint Pesto Pasta

Ingredients:

For the Pesto:

- 1 cup fresh or frozen peas (thawed if frozen)
- 1/2 cup fresh mint leaves, packed
- 1/2 cup grated Parmesan cheese
- 1/4 cup pine nuts or almonds
- 2 cloves garlic, minced
- Juice of 1 lemon
- Salt and pepper to taste
- 1/2 cup extra-virgin olive oil

For the Pasta:

- 12 ounces (about 340g) your favorite pasta (spaghetti, fettuccine, or any shape you prefer)
- Salt for boiling water
- Pea shoots or extra mint leaves for garnish (optional)
- Additional Parmesan cheese for serving

Instructions:

Cook the Pasta:
- Bring a large pot of salted water to a boil.
- Cook the pasta according to the package instructions until al dente.
- Reserve about 1/2 cup of pasta cooking water, then drain the pasta.

Prepare the Pesto:
- In a food processor, combine the peas, mint, Parmesan cheese, pine nuts (or almonds), minced garlic, lemon juice, salt, and pepper.
- Pulse until the ingredients are finely chopped.

Add Olive Oil:
- With the food processor running, slowly pour in the extra-virgin olive oil through the feed tube until the pesto reaches your desired consistency.
- If needed, add some of the reserved pasta cooking water to thin the pesto.

Combine Pesto with Pasta:
- In a large mixing bowl, toss the cooked pasta with the pea and mint pesto until well coated.

Serve:
- Divide the pesto-coated pasta among plates.
- Garnish with pea shoots or extra mint leaves if desired.
- Optionally, sprinkle additional Parmesan cheese on top before serving.

Enjoy:
- Serve immediately and enjoy your Spring Pea and Mint Pesto Pasta!

Feel free to customize the recipe based on your preferences, and you can add extra ingredients like cherry tomatoes, grilled chicken, or roasted vegetables for added flavor and nutrition.

Orange Glazed Carrots

Ingredients:

- 1 pound (about 450g) carrots, peeled and sliced into coins or matchsticks
- 2 tablespoons unsalted butter
- 1/2 cup orange juice (freshly squeezed for best flavor)
- Zest of 1 orange
- 2 tablespoons honey or maple syrup
- Salt and pepper, to taste
- Fresh parsley, chopped (for garnish, optional)

Instructions:

Prepare the Carrots:
- Peel the carrots and cut them into evenly sized coins or matchsticks.

Cook the Carrots:
- In a large skillet or pan, melt the butter over medium heat.
- Add the sliced carrots to the pan and sauté for 2-3 minutes until they start to soften.

Prepare the Glaze:
- In a bowl, mix together the orange juice, orange zest, honey or maple syrup, salt, and pepper.

Glaze the Carrots:
- Pour the orange glaze mixture over the carrots in the pan.

Simmer:
- Reduce the heat to low and let the carrots simmer in the glaze for about 10-15 minutes or until they are tender. Stir occasionally.

Finish and Garnish:
- Once the carrots are tender and the glaze has thickened slightly, remove the pan from heat.
- Garnish with chopped fresh parsley if desired.

Serve:
- Transfer the glazed carrots to a serving dish and drizzle any remaining glaze over the top.
- Serve immediately as a tasty and vibrant side dish.

This orange glazed carrots recipe adds a sweet and citrusy flavor to the carrots, making them a perfect accompaniment to various main dishes. Adjust the sweetness and seasoning according to your taste preferences. Enjoy!

Mini Quiches

Ingredients:

For the Crust:

- 1 1/2 cups all-purpose flour
- 1/2 cup unsalted butter, cold and cubed
- 1/4 teaspoon salt
- 3-4 tablespoons ice-cold water

For the Filling:

- 1 cup milk or heavy cream
- 4 large eggs
- Salt and pepper to taste
- 1 cup grated cheese (cheddar, Swiss, or your choice)
- 1 cup filling ingredients (e.g., diced ham, sautéed mushrooms, spinach, cherry tomatoes, etc.)
- Optional: Fresh herbs like chopped chives or parsley for added flavor

Instructions:

For the Crust:

Prepare the Dough:
- In a food processor, combine the flour, salt, and cubed cold butter. Pulse until the mixture resembles coarse crumbs.
- Add the ice-cold water, one tablespoon at a time, and pulse until the dough comes together.
- Form the dough into a ball, wrap it in plastic wrap, and refrigerate for at least 30 minutes.

Roll and Cut:
- Preheat the oven to 375°F (190°C).
- Roll out the chilled dough on a floured surface and cut circles to fit your mini muffin tin.

Line Muffin Tin:
- Press the dough circles into each mini muffin cup, forming little crusts.

For the Filling:

Prepare the Quiche Filling:
- In a bowl, whisk together eggs, milk or cream, salt, and pepper.
- Stir in the grated cheese and your chosen filling ingredients.

Assemble the Mini Quiches:
- Spoon the filling mixture into each mini crust.

Bake:
- Bake in the preheated oven for 15-20 minutes or until the quiches are set and the crust is golden brown.

Cool and Serve:
- Allow the mini quiches to cool slightly before carefully removing them from the muffin tin.
- Serve warm, garnished with fresh herbs if desired.

Feel free to get creative with the fillings and experiment with different combinations to suit your taste. These mini quiches are great for parties, brunches, or as a tasty snack. Enjoy!

Easter Egg Sugar Cookies

Ingredients:

For the Sugar Cookies:

- 2 3/4 cups all-purpose flour
- 1 teaspoon baking soda
- 1/2 teaspoon baking powder
- 1 cup unsalted butter, softened
- 1 1/2 cups granulated sugar
- 1 large egg
- 1 teaspoon vanilla extract
- 1/2 teaspoon almond extract (optional)
- Pinch of salt

For the Icing:

- 2 cups powdered sugar
- 2-3 tablespoons milk
- 1/2 teaspoon vanilla extract
- Food coloring (assorted colors)
- Sprinkles or edible decorations (optional)

Instructions:

For the Sugar Cookies:

Preheat the Oven:
- Preheat your oven to 375°F (190°C) and line baking sheets with parchment paper.

Combine Dry Ingredients:
- In a medium bowl, whisk together the flour, baking soda, baking powder, and salt. Set aside.

Cream Butter and Sugar:
- In a large bowl, cream together the softened butter and granulated sugar until light and fluffy.

Add Wet Ingredients:
- Beat in the egg, vanilla extract, and almond extract (if using) until well combined.

Incorporate Dry Ingredients:
- Gradually add the dry ingredients to the wet ingredients, mixing until a soft dough forms.

Chill the Dough:
- Divide the dough into two portions, wrap each in plastic wrap, and refrigerate for at least 1 hour.

Roll and Cut:
- Preheat the oven to 375°F (190°C) again.
- Roll out the chilled dough on a floured surface and cut out Easter egg shapes using cookie cutters.

Bake:
- Place the cut-out cookies on the prepared baking sheets and bake for 8-10 minutes or until the edges are lightly golden.

Cool:
- Allow the cookies to cool on the baking sheets for a few minutes before transferring them to a wire rack to cool completely.

For the Icing:

Prepare the Icing:
- In a bowl, whisk together the powdered sugar, milk, and vanilla extract until smooth.

Divide and Color:
- Divide the icing into separate bowls and add food coloring to each bowl, creating the desired colors for decorating.

Decorate:
- Once the cookies are completely cooled, use a small spatula or piping bag to decorate them with the colored icing.

Add Sprinkles (Optional):
- If desired, add sprinkles or other edible decorations to enhance the Easter theme.

Let Icing Set:
- Allow the icing to set before serving or storing the cookies.

These Easter Egg Sugar Cookies are not only delicious but also a fun and creative activity for the whole family. Enjoy making and eating these festive treats!

Honey Mustard Glazed Chicken

Ingredients:

- 4 boneless, skinless chicken breasts
- Salt and pepper to taste
- 1/2 cup Dijon mustard
- 1/4 cup honey
- 2 tablespoons whole grain mustard
- 2 cloves garlic, minced
- 1 teaspoon dried thyme (or 1 tablespoon fresh thyme)
- 2 tablespoons olive oil
- Fresh parsley for garnish (optional)

Instructions:

Preheat the Oven:
- Preheat your oven to 375°F (190°C).

Season Chicken:
- Season the chicken breasts with salt and pepper on both sides.

Prepare the Glaze:
- In a bowl, whisk together Dijon mustard, honey, whole grain mustard, minced garlic, and dried thyme.

Sear the Chicken:
- Heat olive oil in an oven-safe skillet over medium-high heat.
- Sear the chicken breasts for 2-3 minutes on each side until they get a golden brown color.

Apply the Glaze:
- Brush or spoon the honey mustard glaze over each chicken breast, ensuring they are well-coated.

Bake:
- Transfer the skillet to the preheated oven and bake for about 20-25 minutes or until the chicken is cooked through, and the internal temperature reaches 165°F (74°C).

Baste During Cooking:
- Baste the chicken with the glaze from the pan halfway through the cooking time.

Garnish and Serve:
- Remove the chicken from the oven and let it rest for a few minutes.

- Garnish with fresh parsley if desired.

Serve:
- Slice the chicken and serve it with your favorite side dishes, such as roasted vegetables, rice, or a green salad.

This Honey Mustard Glazed Chicken is a crowd-pleaser and perfect for a quick and flavorful dinner. Adjust the sweetness or tanginess by modifying the honey or mustard quantities according to your taste preferences. Enjoy your deliciously glazed chicken!

Cucumber Avocado Salad

Ingredients:

- 2 large cucumbers, peeled and diced
- 2 ripe avocados, diced
- 1/4 red onion, thinly sliced
- 1/4 cup fresh cilantro or parsley, chopped
- Juice of 1-2 limes (adjust to taste)
- 2 tablespoons extra-virgin olive oil
- Salt and pepper to taste
- Optional: Cherry tomatoes, sliced radishes, feta cheese

Instructions:

Prepare the Vegetables:
- Peel and dice the cucumbers.
- Dice the ripe avocados.
- Thinly slice the red onion.
- Chop the fresh cilantro or parsley.

Combine Ingredients:
- In a large bowl, combine the diced cucumbers, diced avocados, sliced red onion, and chopped cilantro or parsley.

Make the Dressing:
- In a small bowl, whisk together the lime juice, extra-virgin olive oil, salt, and pepper. Adjust the lime juice, salt, and pepper to taste.

Dress the Salad:
- Pour the dressing over the cucumber and avocado mixture.

Toss Gently:
- Gently toss the salad to ensure all ingredients are well coated with the dressing.

Optional Additions:
- If desired, add sliced cherry tomatoes, radishes, or crumbled feta cheese for extra flavor and color.

Chill (Optional):
- You can chill the salad in the refrigerator for about 30 minutes to allow the flavors to meld.

Serve:

- Serve the cucumber avocado salad as a side dish or a light and refreshing appetizer.

This salad is not only delicious but also packed with nutrients. The combination of cucumber and avocado provides a satisfying texture and a lovely balance of flavors. Feel free to customize the recipe by adding your favorite herbs or additional vegetables. Enjoy your crisp and creamy Cucumber Avocado Salad!

Lemon Sorbet

Ingredients:

- 1 cup granulated sugar
- 1 cup water
- 1 cup freshly squeezed lemon juice (about 4-6 lemons)
- Zest of 2 lemons
- 1-2 tablespoons vodka or limoncello (optional, helps to keep the sorbet from freezing too hard)
- Pinch of salt

Instructions:

Prepare Simple Syrup:
- In a small saucepan, combine the granulated sugar and water. Heat over medium heat, stirring occasionally, until the sugar completely dissolves. This creates a simple syrup.

Add Lemon Zest:
- Remove the saucepan from heat and add the lemon zest to the simple syrup. Let it steep for about 10-15 minutes to infuse the syrup with lemon flavor. Then, strain out the zest and discard it.

Combine Lemon Juice:
- In a bowl, combine the freshly squeezed lemon juice with the infused simple syrup. Stir well.

Optional: Add Alcohol (Vodka or Limoncello):
- If using, stir in 1-2 tablespoons of vodka or limoncello. This helps prevent the sorbet from freezing too hard.

Chill the Mixture:
- Cover the bowl and refrigerate the lemon mixture for at least 2 hours or until it's thoroughly chilled.

Freeze in Ice Cream Maker:
- Transfer the chilled mixture to your ice cream maker and churn according to the manufacturer's instructions until it reaches a sorbet consistency.

Transfer to a Container:
- Transfer the churned sorbet to a lidded container and freeze for an additional 2-4 hours or until firm.

Serve:
- Scoop the lemon sorbet into bowls or cones and enjoy!

This lemon sorbet is a delightful and palate-cleansing treat. You can also garnish it with a twist of lemon peel or a sprig of mint when serving. Feel free to experiment with other citrus fruits or mix in some berries for different flavor variations. Enjoy your homemade lemon sorbet!

Baked Ziti with Ricotta and Spinach

Ingredients:

- 1 pound (about 450g) ziti pasta
- 1 tablespoon olive oil
- 1 onion, finely chopped
- 3 cloves garlic, minced
- 1 (28-ounce) can crushed tomatoes
- 1 teaspoon dried oregano
- 1 teaspoon dried basil
- Salt and pepper to taste
- 1 package (10 ounces) frozen chopped spinach, thawed and drained
- 2 cups ricotta cheese
- 1 egg, beaten
- 3 cups shredded mozzarella cheese
- 1/2 cup grated Parmesan cheese
- Fresh basil or parsley for garnish (optional)

Instructions:

Preheat your oven to 375°F (190°C).
Cook the ziti pasta according to the package instructions until al dente. Drain and set aside.
In a large skillet, heat olive oil over medium heat. Add chopped onions and cook until softened. Add minced garlic and cook for an additional 1-2 minutes until fragrant.
Pour in the crushed tomatoes and season with dried oregano, dried basil, salt, and pepper. Simmer the sauce for about 15-20 minutes, allowing it to thicken.
In a large mixing bowl, combine the thawed and drained chopped spinach with ricotta cheese. Add the beaten egg and mix well.
In a large baking dish, layer half of the cooked ziti pasta. Spread half of the ricotta and spinach mixture over the pasta, followed by half of the marinara sauce. Sprinkle half of the mozzarella and Parmesan cheeses on top.
Repeat the layers with the remaining ziti, ricotta-spinach mixture, marinara sauce, and cheeses.
Cover the baking dish with aluminum foil and bake in the preheated oven for 25-30 minutes, or until the cheese is melted and bubbly.

Remove the foil and bake for an additional 5-10 minutes or until the cheese on top is golden and slightly crispy.
Allow the baked ziti to cool for a few minutes before serving. Garnish with fresh basil or parsley if desired.

Enjoy your delicious Baked Ziti with Ricotta and Spinach!

Raspberry Lemonade Punch

Ingredients:

- 1 cup fresh raspberries
- 1 cup fresh lemon juice (about 4-6 lemons)
- 1/2 cup granulated sugar (adjust to taste)
- 4 cups cold water
- 2 cups raspberry sorbet or raspberry sherbet
- 3 cups sparkling water or club soda
- Ice cubes
- Lemon slices and fresh mint for garnish (optional)

Instructions:

Prepare Raspberry Lemonade:
- In a blender, combine fresh raspberries, fresh lemon juice, and granulated sugar. Blend until the raspberries are pureed and the mixture is smooth.
- Strain the raspberry-lemon mixture through a fine-mesh sieve into a large pitcher to remove seeds and pulp.

Assemble the Punch:
- To the strained raspberry lemonade, add cold water and stir well to combine.
- Place the pitcher in the refrigerator to chill for at least 1-2 hours.

Serve the Punch:
- Just before serving, add raspberry sorbet or sherbet to the chilled lemonade mixture. Stir gently until the sorbet is partially melted and incorporated.
- Pour in sparkling water or club soda and stir again to combine.

Garnish and Serve:
- Fill glasses with ice cubes and pour the Raspberry Lemonade Punch over the ice.
- Garnish with lemon slices and fresh mint leaves if desired.

Enjoy:
- Serve the Raspberry Lemonade Punch immediately and enjoy the refreshing and fruity flavors.

Feel free to adjust the sweetness by adding more or less sugar according to your taste preferences. You can also get creative by adding fresh berries or citrus slices to enhance the presentation. This punch is sure to be a hit at any party or gathering!

Pecan-Crusted Rack of Lamb

Ingredients:

- 2 racks of lamb (about 1.5 pounds/680g each), Frenched
- Salt and black pepper to taste
- 1 cup pecans, finely chopped
- 1/2 cup breadcrumbs
- 2 tablespoons Dijon mustard
- 2 tablespoons honey
- 2 tablespoons olive oil
- 2 cloves garlic, minced
- 1 tablespoon fresh rosemary, finely chopped
- Fresh mint leaves for garnish (optional)

Instructions:

Preheat the Oven:
- Preheat your oven to 400°F (200°C).

Prepare the Lamb:
- Season the racks of lamb with salt and black pepper. Make sure they are at room temperature for even cooking.

Make the Pecan Coating:
- In a bowl, combine chopped pecans, breadcrumbs, minced garlic, and chopped rosemary. Mix well.

Coat the Lamb:
- Brush the racks of lamb with a thin layer of Dijon mustard. This will help the pecan mixture adhere to the meat.
- Press the pecan mixture onto the lamb racks, ensuring an even coating on all sides.

Sear the Lamb:
- Heat olive oil in an oven-safe skillet over medium-high heat. Sear the lamb racks for 2-3 minutes on each side until they develop a golden-brown crust.

Finish in the Oven:
- Transfer the skillet to the preheated oven and roast the lamb for about 15-20 minutes for medium-rare or longer if you prefer your lamb more well-done. Use a meat thermometer to check for doneness. The internal temperature should reach 130-135°F (54-57°C) for medium-rare.

Prepare the Glaze:
- While the lamb is roasting, mix honey and a bit of Dijon mustard to create a glaze.

Glaze the Lamb:
- Brush the honey-Dijon glaze over the lamb during the last 5 minutes of roasting, allowing it to caramelize slightly.

Rest and Slice:
- Once done, remove the lamb from the oven and let it rest for a few minutes before slicing into individual chops.

Garnish and Serve:
- Garnish with fresh mint leaves if desired and serve the pecan-crusted rack of lamb with your favorite side dishes.

This pecan-crusted rack of lamb is sure to impress with its combination of savory lamb, crunchy pecans, and sweet honey glaze. Enjoy!

Creamy Mushroom and Spinach Tart

Ingredients:

For the Tart Crust:

- 1 1/2 cups all-purpose flour
- 1/2 cup unsalted butter, cold and cubed
- 1/4 cup cold water
- 1/2 teaspoon salt

For the Filling:

- 2 tablespoons olive oil
- 1 onion, finely chopped
- 2 garlic cloves, minced
- 8 ounces (about 225g) mushrooms, sliced (button or cremini mushrooms work well)
- 4 cups fresh spinach, chopped
- Salt and black pepper to taste
- 1 cup heavy cream
- 1/2 cup grated Parmesan cheese
- 1 cup shredded mozzarella cheese
- 3 large eggs
- 1 teaspoon dried thyme (or 1 tablespoon fresh thyme)

Instructions:

Prepare the Tart Crust:
- In a food processor, combine the flour, cold cubed butter, and salt. Pulse until the mixture resembles coarse crumbs.
- Add cold water, one tablespoon at a time, and pulse until the dough comes together.
- Turn the dough out onto a floured surface and shape it into a disk. Wrap it in plastic wrap and refrigerate for at least 30 minutes.

Preheat the Oven:
- Preheat your oven to 375°F (190°C).

Roll out the Tart Crust:
- On a floured surface, roll out the chilled dough into a circle to fit your tart pan. Press the dough into the pan, trimming any excess.

Blind Bake the Crust:
- Line the tart crust with parchment paper and fill it with pie weights or dried beans. Blind bake the crust for about 15 minutes. Remove the weights and parchment paper, then bake for an additional 5 minutes until lightly golden.

Prepare the Filling:
- In a skillet, heat olive oil over medium heat. Add chopped onions and garlic, sauté until softened.
- Add sliced mushrooms and cook until they release their moisture and become golden brown.
- Stir in chopped spinach and cook until wilted. Season with salt and black pepper.

Make the Creamy Filling:
- In a bowl, whisk together heavy cream, Parmesan cheese, shredded mozzarella, eggs, and dried thyme.

Assemble the Tart:
- Spread the mushroom and spinach mixture evenly over the pre-baked tart crust.
- Pour the creamy filling over the vegetables.

Bake the Tart:
- Bake in the preheated oven for 25-30 minutes or until the filling is set and the top is golden brown.

Cool and Serve:
- Allow the tart to cool slightly before slicing. Serve warm and enjoy!

This Creamy Mushroom and Spinach Tart makes for a wonderful appetizer or a light meal, perfect for brunch or a special occasion.

Lemon Poppy Seed Muffins

Ingredients:

- 2 cups all-purpose flour
- 1 cup granulated sugar
- 1 tablespoon poppy seeds
- 1 tablespoon baking powder
- 1/2 teaspoon baking soda
- 1/4 teaspoon salt
- 1 cup plain yogurt or sour cream
- 1/2 cup unsalted butter, melted
- 2 large eggs
- 1 teaspoon vanilla extract
- Zest of 2 lemons
- 2 tablespoons fresh lemon juice

For the Glaze:

- 1 cup powdered sugar
- 2 tablespoons fresh lemon juice
- Zest of 1 lemon

Instructions:

Preheat the Oven:
- Preheat your oven to 375°F (190°C). Line a muffin tin with paper liners.

Mix Dry Ingredients:
- In a large bowl, whisk together the flour, sugar, poppy seeds, baking powder, baking soda, and salt.

Combine Wet Ingredients:
- In another bowl, mix together the yogurt (or sour cream), melted butter, eggs, vanilla extract, lemon zest, and lemon juice.

Combine Wet and Dry Ingredients:
- Pour the wet ingredients into the dry ingredients and gently fold until just combined. Do not overmix; the batter should be lumpy.

Fill Muffin Cups:

- Divide the batter evenly among the muffin cups, filling each about two-thirds full.

Bake:
- Bake in the preheated oven for 18-20 minutes or until a toothpick inserted into the center comes out clean.

Prepare the Glaze:
- While the muffins are baking, prepare the glaze by whisking together powdered sugar, fresh lemon juice, and lemon zest in a bowl until smooth.

Cool and Glaze:
- Allow the muffins to cool in the pan for a few minutes, then transfer them to a wire rack. While the muffins are still warm, drizzle the glaze over the tops.

Serve and Enjoy:
- Let the glaze set before serving. These muffins are best enjoyed fresh but can be stored in an airtight container for a day or two.

These Lemon Poppy Seed Muffins are perfect for breakfast, brunch, or as a sweet treat with your afternoon tea or coffee. Enjoy the burst of citrus flavor!

Roasted Asparagus with Parmesan

Ingredients:

- 1 bunch of fresh asparagus (about 1 pound)
- 2 tablespoons olive oil
- Salt and black pepper to taste
- 1/2 cup grated Parmesan cheese
- Lemon wedges for serving (optional)
- Chopped fresh parsley for garnish (optional)

Instructions:

Preheat the Oven:
- Preheat your oven to 400°F (200°C).

Prepare the Asparagus:
- Wash the asparagus spears and trim the tough ends. You can do this by holding each end and gently bending; the asparagus will naturally snap where it becomes tender.

Coat with Olive Oil:
- Place the trimmed asparagus on a baking sheet. Drizzle olive oil over the asparagus and toss to coat them evenly. Arrange the asparagus in a single layer on the baking sheet.

Season with Salt and Pepper:
- Sprinkle salt and black pepper over the asparagus according to your taste preferences. Toss again to ensure even seasoning.

Roast in the Oven:
- Roast the asparagus in the preheated oven for about 12-15 minutes or until they are tender but still slightly crisp.

Add Parmesan Cheese:
- Sprinkle grated Parmesan cheese over the roasted asparagus during the last 5 minutes of cooking. This allows the cheese to melt and become golden brown.

Serve:
- Once the asparagus is done, transfer them to a serving platter. Squeeze a bit of fresh lemon juice over the asparagus if desired.

Garnish and Enjoy:

- Garnish with chopped fresh parsley for a burst of color and freshness. Serve the Roasted Asparagus with Parmesan immediately.

This dish is not only delicious but also a great way to showcase the natural flavors of asparagus. It pairs well with a variety of main courses and adds a touch of elegance to your meal. Enjoy your Roasted Asparagus with Parmesan!

Easter Bunny Cake

Ingredients:

For the Cake:

- 2 1/2 cups all-purpose flour
- 2 1/2 teaspoons baking powder
- 1/2 teaspoon salt
- 1 cup unsalted butter, softened
- 2 cups granulated sugar
- 4 large eggs
- 1 teaspoon vanilla extract
- 1 cup whole milk

For the Frosting:

- 1 cup unsalted butter, softened
- 4 cups powdered sugar
- 1/4 cup whole milk
- 1 teaspoon vanilla extract

For Decorating:

- Shredded coconut (for bunny fur)
- Pink food coloring (for bunny ears and nose)
- Mini marshmallows (for bunny tail)
- Candy eyes or small chocolate chips (for bunny eyes)
- Pink fondant or icing (for inner ears and mouth)

Instructions:

Preheat the Oven:
- Preheat your oven to 350°F (180°C). Grease and flour two round cake pans.

Prepare the Cake Batter:
- In a medium bowl, whisk together the flour, baking powder, and salt.

Cream Butter and Sugar:
- In a large mixing bowl, cream together the softened butter and granulated sugar until light and fluffy.

Add Eggs and Vanilla:
- Add the eggs one at a time, beating well after each addition. Stir in the vanilla extract.

Combine Dry and Wet Ingredients:
- Gradually add the dry ingredients to the wet ingredients, alternating with the milk. Begin and end with the dry ingredients, mixing until just combined.

Bake the Cake:
- Divide the batter evenly between the prepared cake pans. Bake in the preheated oven for 25-30 minutes or until a toothpick inserted into the center comes out clean. Allow the cakes to cool completely.

Prepare the Frosting:
- In a large mixing bowl, beat together the softened butter, powdered sugar, milk, and vanilla extract until smooth and creamy.

Assemble the Cake:
- Once the cakes are cool, place one layer on a serving plate. Spread a layer of frosting on top. Place the second cake layer on top and frost the entire cake.

Decorate the Easter Bunny:
- Use shredded coconut to cover the bunny's body for fur.
- Tint some coconut with pink food coloring and shape into bunny ears. Place them on top of the cake.
- Create a small pink nose and mouth using pink fondant or icing.
- Add candy eyes or small chocolate chips for the bunny's eyes.
- Place a mini marshmallow for the bunny tail.

Final Touches:
- Add any additional decorations or details you like to personalize your Easter Bunny Cake.

Serve and Enjoy:
- Slice and serve your Easter Bunny Cake to delight your family and friends.

This Easter Bunny Cake makes for a charming centerpiece on your holiday dessert table, and it's a delightful project to involve the family in the Easter festivities. Have fun decorating and celebrating!

Teriyaki Glazed Salmon

Ingredients:

- 4 salmon fillets
- 1/3 cup low-sodium soy sauce
- 3 tablespoons mirin (Japanese sweet rice wine)
- 2 tablespoons sake (or white wine)
- 2 tablespoons brown sugar
- 1 tablespoon honey
- 1 tablespoon rice vinegar
- 1 teaspoon grated fresh ginger
- 2 cloves garlic, minced
- 1 tablespoon cornstarch (optional, for thickening the sauce)
- Sesame seeds and chopped green onions for garnish
- Cooked white rice or steamed vegetables for serving

Instructions:

Prepare the Teriyaki Glaze:
- In a small saucepan, combine soy sauce, mirin, sake, brown sugar, honey, rice vinegar, grated ginger, and minced garlic. Whisk together over medium heat until the sugar is dissolved.

Marinate the Salmon:
- Place the salmon fillets in a shallow dish or a resealable plastic bag. Pour half of the teriyaki glaze over the salmon, ensuring they are well-coated. Marinate for at least 30 minutes in the refrigerator.

Preheat the Oven:
- Preheat your oven to 400°F (200°C).

Bake the Salmon:
- Place the marinated salmon fillets on a baking sheet lined with parchment paper. Bake in the preheated oven for about 12-15 minutes or until the salmon is cooked through and flakes easily with a fork.

Make the Sauce (Optional):
- While the salmon is baking, you can thicken the remaining teriyaki glaze by combining 1 tablespoon of cornstarch with 2 tablespoons of water. Stir this mixture into the saucepan with the reserved teriyaki glaze. Simmer until the sauce thickens slightly.

Glaze the Salmon:
- Brush the baked salmon fillets with the thickened teriyaki glaze during the last few minutes of cooking. This will give the salmon a glossy and flavorful finish.

Serve:
- Transfer the glazed salmon to serving plates. Drizzle any remaining teriyaki glaze over the top. Sprinkle sesame seeds and chopped green onions as garnish.

Enjoy:
- Serve the Teriyaki Glazed Salmon over cooked white rice or with steamed vegetables. Enjoy the delicious flavors!

This teriyaki glazed salmon is a savory and slightly sweet dish that's easy to prepare and perfect for a quick and tasty dinner.

Spring Vegetable Stir-Fry

Ingredients:

- 1 tablespoon vegetable oil
- 1 pound (about 450g) mixed spring vegetables (asparagus, snap peas, baby carrots, bell peppers, broccoli, etc.), washed and chopped
- 2 cloves garlic, minced
- 1 tablespoon fresh ginger, grated
- 1/4 cup soy sauce
- 2 tablespoons oyster sauce
- 1 tablespoon hoisin sauce
- 1 tablespoon rice vinegar
- 1 tablespoon sesame oil
- 1 tablespoon cornstarch (optional, for thickening the sauce)
- 2 green onions, sliced (for garnish)
- Sesame seeds (for garnish)
- Cooked rice or noodles for serving

Instructions:

Prepare the Sauce:
- In a small bowl, whisk together soy sauce, oyster sauce, hoisin sauce, rice vinegar, and sesame oil. If you prefer a thicker sauce, you can mix in 1 tablespoon of cornstarch with 2 tablespoons of water and add it to the sauce.

Heat the Wok or Skillet:
- Heat vegetable oil in a wok or large skillet over medium-high heat.

Sauté Garlic and Ginger:
- Add minced garlic and grated ginger to the hot oil. Stir-fry for about 30 seconds until fragrant.

Stir-Fry Vegetables:
- Add the mixed spring vegetables to the wok. Stir-fry for 3-5 minutes until the vegetables are crisp-tender but still vibrant.

Add the Sauce:
- Pour the prepared sauce over the vegetables. Toss to coat evenly.

Cook Until Vegetables are Tender:

- Continue to stir-fry for an additional 2-3 minutes until the vegetables are cooked to your liking. Be careful not to overcook; you want them to retain their vibrant color and crunch.

Garnish and Serve:
- Sprinkle sliced green onions and sesame seeds over the stir-fry. Toss once more to combine.

Serve Over Rice or Noodles:
- Serve the Spring Vegetable Stir-Fry over cooked rice or noodles.

Enjoy:
- Enjoy this light and flavorful Spring Vegetable Stir-Fry as a quick and healthy meal!

Feel free to customize the vegetables based on what's in season and your preferences. This dish is versatile and a great way to celebrate the fresh flavors of spring.

Strawberry Shortcake

Ingredients:

For the Shortcakes:

- 2 cups all-purpose flour
- 1/4 cup granulated sugar
- 1 tablespoon baking powder
- 1/2 teaspoon salt
- 1/2 cup unsalted butter, cold and cut into small cubes
- 2/3 cup milk
- 1 teaspoon vanilla extract

For the Strawberries:

- 1 pound fresh strawberries, hulled and sliced
- 2-3 tablespoons granulated sugar (adjust according to the sweetness of the strawberries)

For the Whipped Cream:

- 1 cup heavy cream, chilled
- 2 tablespoons powdered sugar
- 1 teaspoon vanilla extract

Instructions:

Preheat the Oven:
- Preheat your oven to 425°F (220°C). Line a baking sheet with parchment paper.

Prepare the Shortcakes:
- In a large bowl, whisk together the flour, sugar, baking powder, and salt. Add the cold cubed butter and use a pastry cutter or your fingers to cut the butter into the dry ingredients until the mixture resembles coarse crumbs.
- In a separate bowl, mix together the milk and vanilla extract. Pour the wet ingredients into the dry ingredients and stir until just combined.

- Turn the dough out onto a floured surface. Gently knead it a few times, then pat it into a 1-inch thick rectangle.
- Using a round cookie cutter or a glass, cut out shortcakes from the dough and place them on the prepared baking sheet.
- Bake for 12-15 minutes or until the shortcakes are golden brown. Allow them to cool on a wire rack.

Prepare the Strawberries:
- In a bowl, combine the sliced strawberries with sugar. Let them sit for about 15-20 minutes, allowing the sugar to macerate the strawberries and create a juicy syrup.

Make the Whipped Cream:
- In a chilled bowl, whip the heavy cream, powdered sugar, and vanilla extract until stiff peaks form.

Assemble the Strawberry Shortcakes:
- Slice the cooled shortcakes in half horizontally. Spoon a generous amount of macerated strawberries onto the bottom half of each shortcake.
- Top the strawberries with a dollop of whipped cream.
- Place the other half of the shortcake on top, creating a sandwich.

Garnish and Serve:
- Garnish with additional whipped cream and a fresh strawberry if desired. Serve immediately and enjoy!

This Strawberry Shortcake recipe is a perfect way to showcase the sweetness of fresh strawberries, paired with tender and slightly sweet shortcakes and fluffy whipped cream. It's a delightful treat for any occasion!

Lemon Garlic Butter Shrimp

Ingredients:

- 1 pound large shrimp, peeled and deveined
- Salt and black pepper, to taste
- 2 tablespoons olive oil
- 4 cloves garlic, minced
- 1/2 teaspoon red pepper flakes (optional, for a bit of heat)
- 1/2 cup chicken or vegetable broth
- Juice of 1 lemon (about 2 tablespoons)
- Zest of 1 lemon
- 3 tablespoons unsalted butter
- 2 tablespoons chopped fresh parsley
- Cooked pasta, rice, or crusty bread for serving

Instructions:

Season the Shrimp:
- Pat the shrimp dry with paper towels. Season them with salt and black pepper according to your taste.

Cook the Shrimp:
- In a large skillet or pan, heat olive oil over medium-high heat. Add the shrimp and cook for 1-2 minutes on each side until they turn pink and opaque. Remove the shrimp from the pan and set them aside.

Sauté Garlic and Red Pepper Flakes:
- In the same pan, add minced garlic and red pepper flakes (if using). Sauté for about 30 seconds until fragrant.

Deglaze with Broth:
- Pour in the chicken or vegetable broth to deglaze the pan, scraping up any browned bits from the bottom.

Add Lemon Juice and Zest:
- Stir in the lemon juice and lemon zest. Allow the mixture to simmer for 1-2 minutes to reduce slightly.

Finish with Butter:
- Reduce the heat to low and add the butter to the pan. Stir until the butter melts and the sauce becomes creamy.

Return Shrimp to the Pan:

- Return the cooked shrimp to the pan, tossing them in the lemon garlic butter sauce. Cook for an additional 1-2 minutes to heat the shrimp through.

Garnish and Serve:
- Stir in chopped fresh parsley for a burst of color and freshness.

Serve:
- Serve the Lemon Garlic Butter Shrimp over cooked pasta, rice, or with crusty bread to soak up the delicious sauce.

Enjoy:
- Enjoy your flavorful and zesty Lemon Garlic Butter Shrimp!

This dish is quick to prepare and has a perfect balance of bright lemon, garlic, and buttery flavors. It's a versatile recipe that pairs well with various side dishes for a complete meal.

Raspberry Lemonade Cupcakes

Ingredients:

For the Cupcakes:

- 1 1/2 cups all-purpose flour
- 1 1/2 teaspoons baking powder
- 1/4 teaspoon salt
- 1/2 cup unsalted butter, softened
- 1 cup granulated sugar
- 2 large eggs
- 1 teaspoon vanilla extract
- Zest of 1 lemon
- 1/2 cup milk
- 1/4 cup fresh lemon juice

For the Raspberry Filling:

- 1 cup fresh or frozen raspberries
- 2 tablespoons granulated sugar
- 1 tablespoon water

For the Lemon Cream Cheese Frosting:

- 8 ounces cream cheese, softened
- 1/2 cup unsalted butter, softened
- 4 cups powdered sugar
- Zest of 1 lemon
- 2 tablespoons fresh lemon juice
- Fresh raspberries for garnish (optional)

Instructions:

Preheat the Oven:
- Preheat your oven to 350°F (175°C). Line a muffin tin with cupcake liners.

Make the Cupcake Batter:
- In a medium bowl, whisk together the flour, baking powder, and salt.

- In a large bowl, cream together the softened butter and sugar until light and fluffy. Add the eggs one at a time, beating well after each addition. Stir in the vanilla extract and lemon zest.
- Gradually add the dry ingredients to the wet ingredients, alternating with the milk and lemon juice. Begin and end with the dry ingredients, mixing until just combined.

Fill Cupcake Liners:
- Divide the batter evenly among the cupcake liners, filling each about two-thirds full.

Bake:
- Bake in the preheated oven for 18-20 minutes or until a toothpick inserted into the center of a cupcake comes out clean.

Make Raspberry Filling:
- While the cupcakes are baking, prepare the raspberry filling. In a small saucepan, combine raspberries, sugar, and water. Cook over medium heat, stirring occasionally, until the raspberries break down and the mixture thickens. Remove from heat and strain to remove seeds.

Core the Cupcakes:
- Once the cupcakes have cooled slightly, use a cupcake corer or a knife to make a hole in the center of each cupcake. Fill the holes with the raspberry filling.

Make Lemon Cream Cheese Frosting:
- In a large bowl, beat together the softened cream cheese and butter until smooth and creamy. Add powdered sugar, lemon zest, and lemon juice. Beat until well combined and fluffy.

Frost the Cupcakes:
- Pipe or spread the lemon cream cheese frosting over the filled cupcakes.

Garnish and Serve:
- Optionally, garnish with fresh raspberries on top.

Enjoy:
- Enjoy your Raspberry Lemonade Cupcakes!

These cupcakes are a delightful treat with a perfect balance of sweet and tangy flavors. They're perfect for spring and summer celebrations or any time you want a burst of refreshing goodness.

Maple Glazed Roasted Carrots

Ingredients:

- 1 pound (about 450g) carrots, peeled and sliced into sticks
- 2 tablespoons olive oil
- Salt and black pepper to taste
- 2 tablespoons maple syrup
- 1 tablespoon Dijon mustard
- 1 tablespoon fresh thyme leaves (optional, for garnish)

Instructions:

Preheat the Oven:
- Preheat your oven to 425°F (220°C).

Prepare the Carrots:
- Peel the carrots and cut them into sticks or coins, ensuring they are similar in size for even cooking.

Coat with Olive Oil:
- In a large bowl, toss the carrot sticks with olive oil, salt, and black pepper until well coated.

Roast the Carrots:
- Spread the seasoned carrots in a single layer on a baking sheet lined with parchment paper. Roast in the preheated oven for 20-25 minutes or until the carrots are tender and slightly caramelized, turning them halfway through.

Prepare the Maple Glaze:
- In a small bowl, whisk together maple syrup and Dijon mustard.

Glaze the Carrots:
- Drizzle the maple syrup mixture over the roasted carrots and toss them to coat evenly. Return the baking sheet to the oven for an additional 5-7 minutes, allowing the glaze to caramelize.

Garnish and Serve:
- Once the carrots are glazed and caramelized to your liking, remove them from the oven. Sprinkle fresh thyme leaves over the top for added flavor and a pop of color.

Serve:

- Transfer the Maple Glazed Roasted Carrots to a serving dish and serve immediately.

Enjoy:
- Enjoy these sweet and savory glazed carrots as a side dish for your favorite meals.

These Maple Glazed Roasted Carrots are not only delicious but also a visually appealing and versatile side dish that pairs well with a variety of main courses. They make a great addition to holiday dinners or weeknight meals.

www.ingramcontent.com/pod-product-compliance
Lightning Source LLC
LaVergne TN
LVHW061943070526
838199LV00060B/3945